How to Become a Crime Scene Investigator

by Sue Hamilton

8/10 21.00

VISIT US AT
WWW.ABDOPUBLISHING.COM

Published by ABDO Publishing Company, 8000 West 78th Street, Suite 310, Edina, Minnesota 55439.
Copyright ©2008 by Abdo Consulting Group, Inc. International copyrights reserved in all countries.
No part of this book may be reproduced in any form without written permission from the publisher.
ABDO & Daughters™ is a trademark and logo of ABDO Publishing Company.

Printed in the United States.

Editor: John Hamilton
Series Consultant: Scott Harr, J.D. Criminal Justice Dept Chair, Concordia University St. Paul
Graphic Design: Sue Hamilton
Cover Design: Neil Klinepier
Cover Illustration: iStockphoto
Interior Photos and Illustrations: p 1 Crime scene investigation, AP; Magnifying glass/print, iStockphoto; p 3 Swab, iStockphoto; p 4 Footprints, iStockphoto; pp 4-5 Investigators search ground, AP; p 6 Evidence bags, iStockphoto; p 7 Detective with evidence, AP; Evidence marker, iStockphoto; p 8 Evidence tag, iStockphoto; *CSI* poster, courtesy CBS Broadcasting Inc.; p 9 Students in mock crime scene, AP; p 10 Tweezers, iStockphoto; CSI Michelle Smith, AP; p 11 Mock crime scene, AP; p 12 Evidence sign, iStockphoto; Skull with bullet hole, AP; p 13 Students at a mock gravesite, AP; p 14 Cherrie Mahan age 8 & age-progressed, AP; p 15 Forensic artist and reconstruction, AP; p 16 Artwork of teeth marks on skin, courtesy U.S. National Library of Medicine; p 17 Forensic dentist examines x-rays, Corbis; p 18 I-35W Bridge collapse, AP; p 19 NTSB officials, courtesy Jeffrey Thompson/Minneapolis Star Tribune; p 20 Fly, iStockphoto; Maggots, ©2007 University of Florida/IFAS/Thomas Wright; p 21 Dr. Jerry Butler, ©2007 University of Florida/IFAS/Thomas Wright; p 22 Forensic pathologist Pornthip Rojanasunand, AP; p 23 Sample autopsy report, AP; p 24 Fingerprint card, Comstock; Dusting for fingerprints, iStockphoto; p 25 Latent print analyst, AP; p 26 Ballistics specialist, Corbis; Bullet casing, iStockphoto; p 27 Three bloodstain patterns, courtesy Norman Reeves, BPA Consulting, Tucson, AZ; Blood spatter patterns test, AP; p 28 CSI photographs evidence, Corbis; Film & media cards, iStockphoto; p 29 Crime scene tape, Corbis; p 30 Fingerprint brush, iStockphoto; p 32 Gloves, iStockphoto.

Library of Congress Cataloging-in-Publication Data

Hamilton, Sue L., 1959-
  How to become a crime scene investigator / Sue Hamilton.
    p. cm. -- (Crime scene investigation)
  Includes index.
  ISBN 978-1-59928-992-2
  1. Criminal investigation--Juvenile literature. 2. Criminal investigation--Vocational guidance--Juvenile literature. 3. Crime scenes--Juvenile literature. 4. Crime scene searches--Juvenile literature. I. Title.
  HV8073.8.H36 2008
  363.25'2--dc22
                              2007035162

CONTENTS

What Does a Crime Scene Investigator Do?

Crime scene investigators (CSIs), also known as a forensic scientists or evidence technicians, search for information and collect physical evidence, such as objects and fluids, at crime scenes. Using these clues, along with the help of science and technology, CSIs assist police investigators in figuring out what happened, when it happened, and who was involved.

It is a job requiring great attention to detail, as well as a strong stomach. CSIs may be asked to work on grim and bloody crime scenes involving murders, assaults, car accidents, and fires. They may also find themselves challenged by old crime scenes, where few clues are to be found. Fortunately, skilled CSIs are trained to know where to look for important pieces of evidence.

CSIs document crime scenes using photography and hand-drawn sketches. They collect fingerprints, take photos, and create molds of footprints. Their job includes finding and collecting hair and fibers, as well as trace evidence. Trace evidence is a small, but measurable, amount of evidence. It can be anything from part of a fingerprint, to a small amount of drugs or explosives, to a tiny drop of blood.

Above: The area where a murder victim was found is searched on hands and knees by crime scene investigators.

Biological fluids are collected by CSIs. These liquids include blood, urine, saliva, and semen. From these samples, DNA, the genetic instruction of all living things, may be extracted in a lab. DNA is like a blueprint, or an instruction manual, that is in every cell of an organism's body. Suspects may be charged with a crime by matching their DNA to samples found at a crime scene.

Besides collecting evidence at crime scenes, CSIs may also work with doctors known as medical examiners, pathologists, or coroners. These professionals determine the cause and manner of a person's death. Crime scene investigators may attend autopsies to assist in collecting evidence from the bodies. Some coroners, especially in rural areas with few people, are not medical doctors. They are local individuals who only confirm that a person is dead. If a person dies under questionable circumstances, a medical doctor is then called in.

Above: Paper and plastic evidence collection bags.

It is important that all items collected at crime scenes or from bodies are done so in a very careful manner. There are rules that CSIs follow when packaging, securing, and even giving evidence to other people working on the case. Breaking the standard procedures and rules could result in evidence being found unusable in court, which means a criminal might go free.

CSIs write detailed reports about their findings. Their collection of information is an important part of solving crimes. They work with police investigators and attorneys, answering questions about what they found while processing a crime scene. It is possible for a CSI to be called to the witness stand during a court trial. A CSI's knowledge of the physical evidence can make or break a case.

Left: A Billings, Montana, police detective carries bags of evidence from a home where a man was shot and killed. Yellow evidence markers indicate other places where CSIs will be collecting evidence.

Below: An evidence marker.

It's NOT Like TV

EVIDENCE IDENTIFICATION

P eople watch the popular TV shows *CSI: Crime Scene Investigation, CSI: Miami,* and *CSI: New York,* along with a number of other similar programs. The shows highlight the important and detailed work of crime scene investigators. However, many parts of these programs are written for entertainment purposes, and do not accurately reflect reality.

On the *CSI* programs, the main characters not only investigate and collect evidence, they also use lab equipment to conduct tests and solve cases. While a CSI may do all of these jobs, often their real world work is more specific. Usually, a CSI's job is to collect, bag, and label evidence at a crime scene. Some evidence is given to lab specialists, who test and identify what has been collected. All of the information is turned over to police detectives, who take the facts and details collected by CSIs and then proceed with their investigations.

In the past, most CSIs were police officers. Before they took on the job of CSI, they already had hundreds of hours of crime scene experience. Today, there are a number of schools that offer criminal justice and forensic science degrees to people who want to be CSIs, but don't necessarily want to become police officers.

Above Right: A poster for the popular CBS TV show *CSI: Crime Scene Investigation. Above Left:* An evidence identification tag.

However, many law enforcement agencies prefer to have the additional knowledge a police officer brings to the CSI job. Each state, even each police station, is different.

The CSI television programs do try to present some of the horror and gruesomeness of violent and tragic crime scenes.

Above: A pretend crime scene is set up at Penn State College in State College, Pennsylvania. The crime scene lab has been created to help teach forensic science students.

Seeing a TV crime scene from the comfort and safety of a person's own living room is nothing like being faced with the real thing. Carl Williams, an experienced CSI and former police detective, stated in a Florida newspaper interview, "Crime scene investigation is not a job for everyone. The television shows are for entertainment, not reality. The crime scene doesn't wrap up in an hour, never mind an entire investigation. That can take months. Also, television doesn't show the real horror of what one human being can do to another. Not a lot of people can stomach it. But if you can take it, the job can be fascinating work."

Forensic Skills & Education

Below: Crime scene investigator Michelle Smith holds a master's degree in sociology with an emphasis on criminology from Arkansas State University.

The word "forensics" is defined as using science and technology to investigate a crime and provide facts in a court of law. A CSI's job is to collect the puzzling pieces of a crime. They work in all types of weather—extreme heat, cold, wind, and rain. It is often difficult, gruesome, smelly, and complicated work. CSIs needs to be logical, patient, and determined to find answers. They must remain impartial and objective—the information they uncover may help the police, or it may help suspects defend themselves.

Often the best way to become a CSI is to first study and train as a police officer. This education and experience lets investigators who have spent time at crime scenes move into the field of evidence collection or analysis. In addition, towns and cities that do not have the money to hire both police officers and CSIs often have officers perform both jobs.

Some CSIs who work in large cities, with bigger budgets and higher crime rates, have very specific jobs with special training requirements. Many people without police training turn to colleges and universities for their education.

Several schools have programs that have been approved by the American Academy of Forensic Sciences. Some jobs require one or two years of additional study after high school. Other positions require four-year college degrees in chemistry, biology, or science. Still others require extended training beyond college. Even after a person has the education, he or she then needs to be trained by their employer, a law enforcement agency.

Above: A police patrolman examines a mock crime scene set up to help train field investigators in Roswell, New Mexico.

Paul Friedman, a former CSI and current professor of the Criminal Justice Department of Florida's Palm Beach Community College, said, "The trend has been to put civilians in the field. In the past, police officers would examine the scene and collect evidence. Now, there are still some sworn officers on the scene. It depends on the individual department's preference."

Forensic Science Jobs

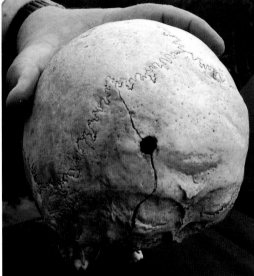

Above: A skull with a bullet hole wound in the back.

There are many different forensic science job areas. According to Professor Paul Friedman, "Crime scene technologists enter the field to find, collect, preserve, and document the evidence. They spend a good amount of time reconstructing the scene. But then they turn the evidence over to another type of expert for analysis."

Forensic specialists do not work alone. Forensic pathologists examine corpses to determine a cause of death. Forensic entomologists look at the bugs found on dead bodies and use their knowledge of insects to determine when, and even where, a person died. Forensic dentists use their knowledge of teeth to help identify dead bodies. Forensic anthropologists may be called to examine bones of human remains.

It is said that the dead tell no tales, but the clues surrounding them often do. Here are a few of the many specialists who work in different forensic areas.

Forensic Anthropologist

If there's a skeleton, decomposed corpse, burned, mummified, mutilated, or dismembered body at a crime scene, it's likely that a forensic anthropologist will be called in to help. Often with the little evidence, usually only bones or burned human remains, forensic anthropologists use their knowledge of how people live to find out how they might have died.

EVIDENCE

Forensic anthropologists also use their knowledge of human bodies to help discover who a person was, and sometimes what he or she looked like.

Forensic anthropologists know that bones are excellent clues. A skull or pelvis bone can help tell whether a body belonged to a man or a woman. The ends of rib bones, which wear down the tiniest bit every time a person takes a breath, help identify a person's age. The length of leg bones, and sometimes even arm bones, help determine height. Facial bones, such as the shape of eye sockets and cheekbones, can determine a person's race.

There are only a few forensic anthropologists in the world. Less than 100 of these professionals are certified with the American Board of Forensic Anthropology. Law enforcement agencies call on these specialists on a case-by-case basis, usually when a crime appears to have taken place.

Below: Two students with the Armed Forces DNA Identification Laboratories in Maryland, and one from the Salt Lake City Police Department, remove bones from a mock gravesite as part of a training exercise.

Forensic Artist

Trying to identify a decomposed body is difficult. A law enforcement agency could never send out a picture of a skull with bits of flesh attached and a headline: "Do you know this person?" Nearly as difficult is getting accurate descriptions of criminals. Victims often only see their attackers for a few terrifying seconds. Getting them to remember any facial or body details requires a professional who knows how to ask the right questions. That's where the challenging skills of a forensic artist comes in, a job that mixes art, science, and communication.

Forensic artists have four main jobs. First, they create artistic drawings of suspects. This is known as composite imagery. Specific parts of a face are described to the artist and then brought together into one image. The artist may use a pencil and paper or a computer program to do this. These same techniques are used in another part of their job: reconstructive or postmortem drawings. With a skull and whatever clues were found at the crime scene, such as clothing or hair, an artist tries to recreate a face, with the hope that someone will recognize the dead person. Forensic artists may even use clay to sculpt a face right on the skull.

Forensic artists are often asked to create demonstrative evidence for use in court. This can include drawings or computer-generated artwork showing information from a crime.

Image modification/identification is a task in which forensic artists change how a person looks. For example, if someone has been missing for years, the artist takes what a person looked like when he or she was last seen, then "ages" the person to create an image of what that person might look like today. In addition, a forensic artist may be asked to draw a disguised suspect, changing the criminal's hairstyle or hair color.

Below: Missing child Cherrie Mahan, a girl last seen at the age of 8, is shown as she looked in 1985 and age-progressed to show her as a 23-year-old woman.

Above: Forensic artist and Michigan State Trooper Sarah Foster reconstructed the face of Shawn Patrick Raymond. Trooper Timothy Brown, standing in the background, remembered the boy as a missing person and identified him.

Left: In the course of an investigation, a forensic dentist will sometimes be asked to look at bite marks left on the skin of victims by attackers or, reversely, the bite marks that victims have left on attackers. An odontologist may be able to identify who left the bites.

Forensic Dentist

Teeth are often used to help identify corpses. Unlike soft tissue, such as skin and muscle, teeth will often survive explosions, fires, severe accidents, underground burial, and even soaking in water. It's the job of a forensic dentist, also known as a forensic odontologist, to examine a body's teeth and use dental records, x-rays, and photographs to help identify a victim's remains. Sometimes a forensic dentist will have as little as a single tooth to work with, but may still be able to tell investigators the estimated age of the tooth's owner.

Forensic dentists may also be asked to look at bite marks left by attackers or victims. By looking at the bites, a forensic dentist may be able to match the marks to the teeth of a suspect or victim. However, experienced professionals are quick to note that this type of identification is not necessarily 100 percent accurate. Dr. Richard Souviron, chief forensic odontologist at Florida's Miami-Dade Medical Examiner's office, said, "If you say that this bite fits this person and nobody else in the world, and if you use the bite mark as the only piece of physical evidence linking an attacker to his victim, that's not science—that's junk." A bite mark, like so much other forensic evidence, is just one piece to a larger puzzle in solving a crime.

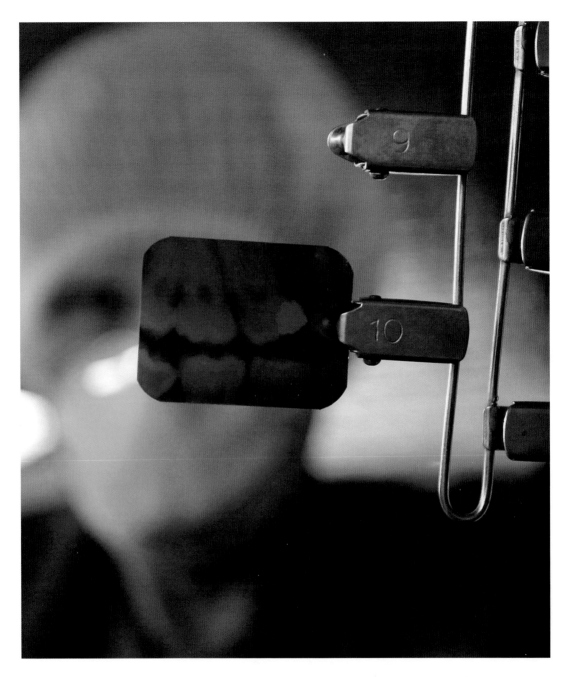

Above: A forensic dentist looks at dental x-rays to try to identify a victim. While the soft tissue of a body decomposes fairly quickly, especially in warm climates, teeth may stay intact. A forensic dentist will often be called in to identify a victim based on the remaining teeth.

Below: On August 1, 2007, the I-35W bridge in Minneapolis, Minnesota, collapsed. Thirteen lives were lost.

Forensic Engineer

From a one-person traffic accident caused by faulty brakes to a bridge collapse resulting in the deaths and injuries of many people, it is the job of a forensic engineer to find out what happened. Forensic engineers take their knowledge of how things work to uncover why mechanical items fail. This research is used in court trials.

A forensic engineer's job is to conduct a root cause analysis—finding out the real cause of an accident. For example, after a driver reports brake failure, the forensic engineer will look at the car's brakes to see if they were poorly designed. Or perhaps the brakes were good, but they were installed incorrectly. Or perhaps the driver reported failed brakes as an excuse, but really was simply not watching the road.

Above: In October 2007, engineering experts from the National Transportation Safety Board (NTSB) inspected wreckage of the fallen I-35W bridge. The officials were trying to discover what caused the bridge to fall two months earlier.

A forensic engineer would examine the brakes, as well as the vehicle's damage, plus go to the scene of the accident to figure out exactly what happened—the root cause.

In the case of a bridge collapse, a forensic engineer will look at how and when the bridge was built, what materials were used in its construction, as well as how well it was maintained, how many cars traveled over it, what the weather was like when it collapsed, and many other factors. A forensic engineer, using knowledge of how things work as well as extreme attention to detail, dissects an accident to find an answer.

Forensic Entomologist

For some people, the idea of searching for bugs on a dead body sounds awful, but for a forensic entomologist, these small creatures provide excellent clues to a case. A forensic entomologist can often tell how long a body has been decomposing based on the bugs found on the corpse. Flies, maggots, beetles, mites, and moths all move in on dead bodies at various times. For example, if blowfly eggs are found, it usually means that the body has been dead for approximately two days.

A forensic entomologist must know a great deal about arthropods, which include insects and spiders: where they live, what they eat, how long it takes for their eggs to hatch, and how long they live.

Bugs can help investigators tell where a crime has been committed. For example, if a certain kind of insect is found on a body, but that insect is normally found in another state or region, the forensic entomologist might conclude that the body has been moved sometime after the murder.

Bugs may even help identify killers. In 1982, chigger bites were found on a man suspected of murdering a woman in Ventura County, California. Chiggers are tiny mites that live on or under the skin and leave red, itchy bite marks. Some investigators working near the woman's corpse, which was found underneath a eucalyptus tree, discovered that they, too, had chigger bites. A forensic entomologist analyzed the bites and connected the suspect to the crime, since only those people who were in the same exact area as the body had chigger bites. This piece of evidence helped convict the suspect of murder.

Above: Flies are usually the first insects to find a corpse.

Below: A forensic entomologist measures the size of blowfly maggots to estimate how long they have been on a dead body.

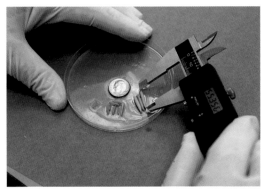

Above: Dr. Jerry Butler, a forensic entomologist from the University of Florida, examines blowfly larvae taken from a murder victim.

Along with assisting in murder investigations, forensic entomologists also search for bugs found in food and in homes. These insects may infest certain products, which can cause people to get sick.

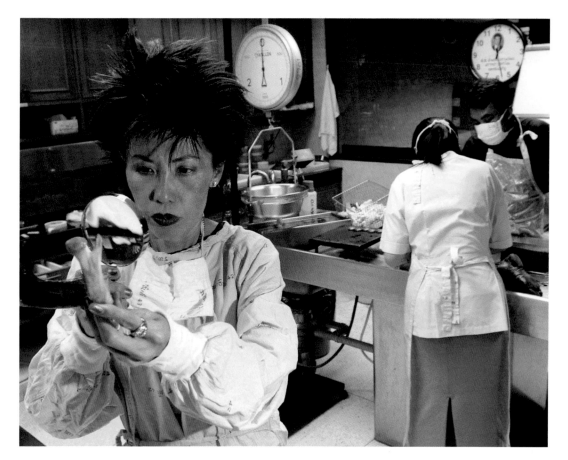

Above: Famous forensic pathologist Pornthip Rojanasunand examines a human bone.

Forensic Pathologist

A man's body (we'll call him John Doe) arrives at a morgue with a bullet wound in his leg, a bee sting on his hand, and an open wound on the back of his head. What killed him? It's up to the forensic pathologist, a doctor who examines a body, to discover the exact cause of death.

The job of a forensic pathologist requires a lot of training. First, a person must become a medical doctor, which takes about eight years. That person must then be trained in anatomical pathology, which explains the causes and effects of diseases on bodies. Finally, in the United States, a forensic pathologist must pass a test and be registered with the American Board of Pathology. Several other countries have similar testing requirements.

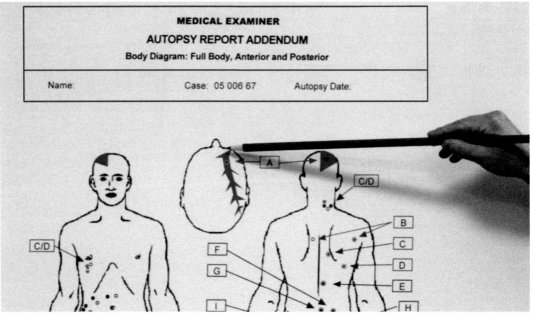

MEDICAL EXAMINER

AUTOPSY REPORT ADDENDUM

Body Diagram: Full Body, Anterior and Posterior

Name: Case: 05 006 67   Autopsy Date:

Once trained, a forensic pathologist has the skills to perform an autopsy on a body to find out what killed that person. In the case of John Doe, police investigators guessed that the man bled to death from the bullet wound, or that a blow to the back of his head caused death. But the forensic pathologist determined that it was a bee sting that killed him. Recreating the scene, it was determined that the man was a hunter who had been stung on his hand. He was very allergic to bee venom. He tried to get back to his car, where he had a bee-sting kit. Very quickly, however, the man found it difficult to breathe. He began to lose consciousness, fell, and dropped his gun. The gun discharged. The bullet hit a rock and ricocheted, or rebounded, hitting the man in the leg. The trauma to the back of his head happened when he collapsed, hitting a large rock on the ground.

By understanding the effects of bee venom on the human body, the forensic pathologist was able to pinpoint the man's cause of death as an accident and alert investigators. No crime had taken place.

Above: A sample autopsy report showing multiple wounds found on a murder victim.

23

Specialists in the Field

Above: A fingerprint card.

here are some forensic jobs that are very specialized. These jobs are often part of what a forensic scientist does on a day-to-day basis, but some CSIs have additional training and knowledge to become specialists.

Fingerprint Analyst

A fingerprint analyst's job is to positively identify people by their fingerprints. A fingerprint shows the patterns—the lines and whorls—on the pad of a person's finger. The same is true of a person's toes. The raised parts of the skin are known as friction ridges. Each person's prints are unique to them—even identical twins. Fingerprints do not change over time. Fingerprint analysts collect and study three different types of prints at crime scenes: latent, patent, and plastic.

A latent print is one that is hidden from the eye. It becomes visible by using powders, chemicals, or electronic processes. There may be many problems with this type of print. It is the most difficult type of print to identify. Only part of the print may be visible, or it may be blurred or twisted out of shape.

A patent print is one that is visible to the eye. Blood, oil, paint, ink, or some other substance gets on a finger and is then pressed onto another surface, such as a counter, floor, or window. Since the print is clear and visible, this type of print is usually photographed.

Below: Dusting for latent fingerprints on a door handle.

24

A plastic print is one where the finger's friction ridges actually show up in a soft material that retains the patterns and shapes of the finger. Plastic prints can be found in wax, clay, or even oil. In addition to photographing plastic prints, analysts also look for additional fingerprints under the ones that are clearly visible.

Fingerprint analysts can use prints to identify dead bodies. They may be asked to find the name of a suspect or a victim from a print. When a crime is committed, suspects are fingerprinted by placing their inked fingertips on a small card. There are millions of these cards in existence, most of which have been scanned and placed in a computer system. Some have not. An analyst may have to search through thousands of fingerprint cards to identify a victim or suspect.

The job of a fingerprint analyst requires patience, as well as excellent eyesight and memory. Fingerprint analysts may be called into court to testify, and must be able to show how they've identified a print belonging to a specific person.

Below: A latent print analyst sits by a computer showing a side-by-side comparison of a fingerprint lifted from a crime scene and a print from a police database.

Right: A forensic firearms investigator studies grooves on a .223 slug on an Integrated Ballistics Identification System (IBIS) at the National Lab Center in Rockville, Maryland. *Below:* A .45 bullet casing photographed next to a millimeter ruler. Ballistics specialists are often able to tell if a bullet or shell casing was fired from a certain gun by the scratches unique to each gun's barrel.

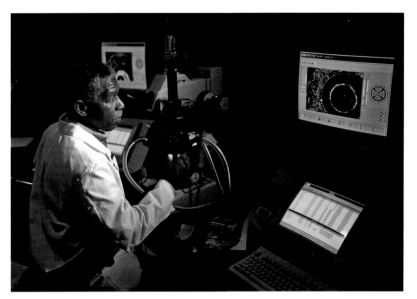

Ballistics Specialist

Guns often play a major role in crime scene investigations. Ballistics is a science that studies how bullets, cartridges, and guns work. A ballistics specialist analyzes how firearms are used in crimes. These forensic scientists can often tell if a bullet or shell casing has been fired from a specific gun. Ballistics specialists may also be asked to conduct firing tests to see if a bullet, which may have changed shape after passing into or through a person or nearby object, came from a certain firearm.

Gunpowder testing on suspects, however, is used more in entertainment than in the real world of crime scene investigators. Today's guns use smokeless powder that leaves only traces of nitrates—chemicals that are a combination of oxygen, nitrogen, and other elements. There are tests available to look for nitrates, but such common products as fertilizer, ammonia, and dishwashing detergents also contain these chemicals. A positive test proves little.

Modern ballistics specialists may spend little time searching for gunpowder residue, but their skills are definitely in demand to positively match weapons and their projectiles.

Bloodstain Pattern Analyst

A bloodstain pattern analyst, also called a BPA, views a crime scene and provides a description of what happened based on the blood found, such as spray patterns on a wall, or pooling on a floor. Norman Reeves, a forensic consultant in Tucson, Arizona, says, "Possible and impossible scenarios may be established to determine if the victim or witness or assailant is accurately describing what took place."

BPAs may be able to find out such things as the type of weapon used, where the attacker and victim were when the violence took place, how many times a person was struck with a weapon, and whether the bloodstain patterns match the findings of other professionals working on the case, such as the detectives and the medical examiner.

BPAs prefer to go directly to crime scenes, but they may also be called in months later to examine crime scene photographs, evidence, or videos, especially if there are conflicting reports between victims and attackers. A bloodstain pattern analyst can often find the truth based on what is seen on floors, walls, windows, clothing, vehicles, and other objects.

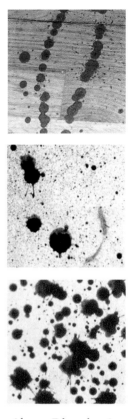

Above: Bloodstain patterns: passive drops from gravity, gunshot spatter, beating spatter.
Left: A CSI classroom demonstration of blood spatter patterns is prepared using sterile blood on a sponge and a pipe.

Forensic Photographer

Forensic photographers are often the first CSIs to enter a secured crime scene. In extreme heat and fierce cold, light and dark, inside and outside, photographers thoroughly document everything from the general area to the smallest evidence. Their work details exactly how

Above: A crime scene investigator photographs evidence.

Below: The film rolls or memory cards forensic photographers use to document a crime scene are entered into case files as evidence.

a scene looks immediately after a crime is discovered, before investigators or evidence collectors have arrived.

This is a detailed and exacting science. Photographs are taken of the general crime scene area, including street signs. Photos are then shot of nearby streets, alleys, vehicles, fields, and trees. If there are tire marks in the street, those are photographed. The front, back, and sides of buildings, and any doors or windows where an attacker, victim, or witness may have entered or exited are documented.

If a crime scene is inside a building, photos are needed to show an overall picture of where the crime took place. If the crime is a murder or suicide, close-ups are shot of the body, the body's location, and any marks, bites, or skin impressions.

Next comes evidence. Photos are taken of such objects as weapons, bullets, bullet casings, fingerprints, footprints, shoe prints, dropped items, and anything else that may be important. Plus, most evidence photos are shot twice. The second time a small ruler is placed in the scene to show the size and/or location of the item.

Photographers may also be asked to videotape the scene, using the camera to provide an unbroken sweep of the crime scene and surrounding area. The forensic photographer's work is frequently used in court. Both sides of a trial, the prosecutor and the defendant, often depend on the forensic photographer's work to help prove their case.

EVIDENCE

Are Forensic Sciences for Everyone?

Not everyone can stand the work that crime scene investigators undertake. Not only do they work all hours of the day and night under some of the harshest conditions, CSIs also see many horrors in their work. However, for people who love logic and science, find satisfaction helping to put criminals in jail (or keep innocent people out of jail), and want a different challenge every day, then becoming a crime scene investigator may be the right work for them.

Below: Crime scene tape marks an area in which CSIs look for evidence. It's a challenging and sometimes gruesome job, but one with many rewards.

GLOSSARY

ARSON — A crime where a person purposely sets fire to property.

ARTHROPODS — A group of animals that includes insects, spiders, and crustaceans. Arthropods have an external skeleton, a segmented body, and jointed limbs.

ASSAILANT — A person who attacks another person.

AUTOPSY — An exam performed on a dead body to find out the cause of death.

CORPSE — A dead body.

DECOMPOSE — A process that happens after death when a body begins to rot, breaking down into its most basic elements.

DEFENDANT — A person, business, or entity (such as a corporation or town) accused of doing something wrong. In a court trial, defendants try to defend themselves against the charge or charges placed against them.

DISMEMBER — To separate an arm or leg from a body.

DNA — DNA stands for the scientific term Deoxyribonucleic Acid. In living things, DNA is the material inside the center of every cell that forms genes. This material is inherited from a person's or other living thing's parents. Except for identical twins, each person's DNA is unique to that person. Identical twins have identical DNA.

EVIDENCE — Objects, and sometimes information, that helps prove the details and facts in a legal investigation.

GRAND THEFT — Stealing something that is valued at more than $400. This may include money, cars, boats, jewelry, or other expensive items or services.

IMPARTIAL — Fair and objective. Not favoring one side or the other.

INFEST — Large numbers of bugs or other unwanted animals invade places or products where they create an unhealthy situation.

LARVAE — The worm-like form of many insects when they are newly hatched, prior to the bugs changing into their winged, adult shape.

MAGGOT — The soft-bodied, legless larvae of a blowfly or housefly, usually found in decaying tissue.

MEDICAL EXAMINER — A medical doctor authorized to find the cause of death of bodies whose deaths are not related to natural causes.

MORGUE — A place where dead bodies are stored until they are identified and claimed by family members or until arrangements are made for burial.

MUTILATE — Badly injured, often violently.

POSTMORTEM — After death.

PROJECTILE — An object that is moved through the air using force. This usually refers to objects fired from a weapon, such as bullets or arrows, but it can also mean such things as balls or rocks.

PROSECUTOR — A person who brings charges of wrongdoing against another person, business, or government entity. These charges may lead to a trial taking place. During this trial, the prosecution will try to prove that the defendant is guilty.

INDEX